MELISSA GREENE

Michigan Hikes
Guide to 40 Walks & Hikes

Copyright © 2024 by Melissa Greene

All rights reserved. No part of this publication may be reproduced, stored or transmitted in any form or by any means, electronic, mechanical, photocopying, recording, scanning, or otherwise without written permission from the publisher. It is illegal to copy this book, post it to a website, or distribute it by any other means without permission.

Melissa Greene asserts the moral right to be identified as the author of this work.

Melissa Greene has no responsibility for the persistence or accuracy of URLs for external or third-party Internet Websites referred to in this publication and does not guarantee that any content on such Websites is, or will remain, accurate or appropriate.

Designations used by companies to distinguish their products are often claimed as trademarks. All brand names and product names used in this book and on its cover are trade names, service marks, trademarks and registered trademarks of their respective owners. The publishers and the book are not associated with any product or vendor mentioned in this book. None of the companies referenced within the book have endorsed the book.

First edition

This book was professionally typeset on Reedsy. Find out more at reedsy.com

Contents

Introduction	1
Selecting A Trail	3
Preparation	5
Northern Lower Peninsula Trails	7
Southern Lower Peninsula Trails	14
Eastern Upper Peninsula Trails	18
Western Upper Peninsula Trails	22
Conclusion	27
Resources	28

Introduction

Welcome to Michigan Hikes Guide! My name is Melissa Greene, I'm very excited to be writing this guide book. I plan on using it myself to explore Michigan. I have a strong passion for being outside and enjoying nature. Hiking is a great way to reset myself and get some exercise at the same time. Michigan is a very beautiful place to venture outdoors. There are a variety of amazing scenes and the different seasons add to their beauty.

  I was born and raised in Michigan and I am still amazed at how beautiful it is here throughout the different seasons. I lived away for many years due to Military obligations. I have learned from my travels and meeting many people from all over the world, that not everyone knows that Michigan has an Upper and a Lower Peninsula. I bring this up now because it is important to know when planning your hikes. This guide book sorts them out by the Peninsulas and different regions throughout. Hopefully, this will be helpful for everyone.

  This guide is a gathering of different trails in Michigan that I compiled for people to use. Please verify online before planning your trip for possible closures and changes to trails.

  Please be safe and use caution while hiking. Hiking is a sport that can be enjoyable and refreshing. Rushing through a trail could possibly cause an injury. Be aware of your surroundings at all times and make sure that you do not go off of the trail. There may be roots from trees that can cause a tripping hazard, especially if they are covered with downed leaves. Do not ignore signs posted for your safety. Also the different wildlife that you may encounter is something that you should be prepared for. The trails might be marked if there is a possibility of bears to look out for. One very important thing to find out is the hunting seasons and know which trails are on possible hunting grounds. Some trails are protected from hunting but not all of them. As mentioned earlier, it is important to go online before planning your trip to make an informed decision on the selection of your trails.

Selecting A Trail

Deciding on which trail to select may not seem difficult for some people. It is important to put some thought in selecting the appropriate trail to take. Here are some of the things that should be considered in your decision:

Location- Traveling to the trail may take some of the daylight hours. This is important for longer trail distances. Plan your time accordingly to finish the hike before sunset. Keeping in mind that some trails might not be marked clearly.

Weather- This could cause the trails to be slippery and affect visibility as well.

Trail length- Important to consider the endurance and strength of those going on the trail with you.

Level of Difficulty- There are different levels due to distance, grade, and terrain.

Elevation- The air is thinner at higher elevations and could affect some people with breathing difficulty i.e. asthma.

Equipment required- The appropriate equipment is an important thing to consider. It is always best to be prepared.

Pets- Some trails allow pets on a leash. It is important to verify online and check if your pet will be able to handle the distance and terrain that will be encountered.

Required entry fees- There may be entry fees to access a trail. Check online for the current costs per vehicle or person, when on foot or bicycle. Some State Parks require the Michigan Recreation passport for vehicle entry.

Disclaimer

The author and publisher of this guidebook shall not be held liable for any loss, injury, damage, or inconvenience from the use of the information provided. Hikers are advised to obtain up-to-date trail maps, weather forecasts, and safety information before embarking on any hike, and to adhere to local regulations and guidelines.

By using this guidebook, you acknowledge and agree that hiking can involve possible risks, and that you are solely responsible for your own safety and well-being while on the trail. Always exercise caution, use common sense, and be prepared for unexpected circumstances when hiking in any outdoor environment.

Preparation

Please keep in mind that some trails may be closed for various reasons. There might also be changes with trails after writing this book. It would be best to check online while planning your trip.

Recommended supplies

It is always good practice to be prepared for the various hikes that you will go on. Here is a list of just a few suggested items to bring on your hike.

- Map of trail- it is possible that some trails are not marked well (best to download it before traveling, maps might not be available on site)
- Water (Quantity should be appropriate for the distance and temperature)
- Food or snacks
- Comfortable shoes with good tread (to avoid slipping)
- Hat (appropriate for weather conditions)
- Outerwear (appropriate for weather conditions)
- Backpack of some kind to carry items securely
- Hiking poles
- Compass/GPS
- Portable charger for cell phone

- Sunblock
- Insect repellent of some sort (Some trails could be uncomfortable without this. Mosquitoes and black flies are something to be prepared for with the various trails.)
- Clothing to avoid insect bites or ticks

If you have found this book helpful, I'd be very appreciative if you left a favorable review for the book on Amazon! Happy Hiking! Thank you!

Northern Lower Peninsula Trails

Agnes S. Andreae Nature Preserve Loop (Easy, 1.4 miles, Elevation gain 183 ft)

This beautiful trail is in Afton, Michigan. The route type is a loop along the lower Pigeon River and is 1.4 miles. Some of the many things that can be enjoyed while visiting this trail are hiking, walking and wildlife. The different seasons enhance the views of the forest and Pigeon River. Be prepared for mosquitos, woods and water are a combination that mosquitos may be an issue. Bringing some form of insect repellent is suggested. Pets are allowed on a leash.

Cheboygan State Park Green, Black, and Blue Trail - Shore Loop (Easy, 4.1 miles, Elevation gain 26 ft)

This trail is near Cheboygan, Michigan. The route type is a loop and is 4.1 miles. It goes through the woods, sand dunes and a beach on the shoreline of Lake Huron. There is almost a mile of the trail that you will be walking in the sand. Plan to have appropriate shoes for the sand and possible ticks. Some of the many things that can be enjoyed while visiting this trail are hiking, walking, mountain biking, bird watching, fishing, camping and wildlife. The different seasons enhance the views of the lake, forest, and wildflowers. Be prepared for mosquitos, woods and water are a combination that mosquitos may be an issue. Bringing some form of insect repellent is suggested. Michigan Recreation Passport is required for vehicle entry. Pets are allowed on a leash.

Deadman's Hill (Moderate, 3.1 miles, Elevation gain 419 ft)

This trail is near Elmira Township, Michigan. The route type is a loop and is 3.1 miles. The trailhead is the highest point of the trail. Going on the trail counter clockwise is suggested so that the beginning will be a steep decline and the end of the trail will not be as steep of an incline. This is a beautiful hike with views of the Jordan River watershed. There is a viewpoint along the trail as well. Some of the many things that can be enjoyed while visiting this trail are hiking, walking, running, bird watching, and wildlife. The different seasons enhance the views of the beautiful wildflowers. The fall time is so amazing with the variety of colors. Best traveled in May through November. Pets are allowed on a leash.

Empire Bluff Trail (Moderate, 1.5 miles, Elevation gain 170 ft)

Located in Sleeping Bear Dunes National Lakeshore, Empire, Michigan. The route type is out and back and is 1.5 miles. Be prepared for sand on parts of this trail. Use caution for slopes and do not ignore posted signs. The trail will lead to a spectacular view of Lake Michigan. Some of the many things that can be enjoyed while visiting this trail are hiking, walking, running, bird watching, and wildlife. Pets are allowed on a leash. It is important to verify online and check if your pet will be able to handle the distance and terrain that will be encountered. There is an entry fee by vehicle or if by foot per person.

Fisherman's Island Nature Trail (Easy, 5.9 miles, Elevation gain 272 ft)

This trail is in Fisherman's Island State Park, near Charlevoix, Michigan. The route type is out and back and is 5.9 miles. There are beautiful views of hills and Lake Michigan. Some of the many things that can be enjoyed while visiting this trail are hiking, running, camping, bird watching, wildflowers, wildlife and forest. Be prepared for mosquitos, woods and water are a combination that mosquitos may be an issue. Bringing some form of insect repellent is suggested. The trail is best traveled April through October. Vault toilets are available. Michigan Recreation Passport is required for vehicle entry.

Lakeshore Drive (Easy, 3.8 miles, Elevation gain 42 ft)

This trail is in Fisherman's Island State Park near Charlevoix, Michigan. The route type is out and back and is 3.8 miles. There are views of Lake Michigan and the beautiful shoreline. Some of the many things that can be enjoyed while visiting this trail are hiking, running, wildlife and forest. Pets are allowed on a leash. Michigan Recreation Passport is required for vehicle entry.

Ocqueoc Falls (Easy, 0.3 miles, Elevation gain 13 ft)

This trail is part of Mackinaw State Forest near Millersburg, Michigan. The route type is out and back and is only .3 mile. This trail can be busy, possibly because of the length and convenience. This trail is best traveled May through October. The fall colors will always make it an exceptional time to visit Ocqueoc Falls. Some of the many things that can be enjoyed while visiting this trail are hiking, walking and bird watching. Be prepared for mosquitos, woods and water are a combination that mosquitos may be an issue. Bringing some form of insect repellent is suggested. Restrooms are available at the parking lot. Pets are allowed on a leash.

Besser State Natural Area (Easy, 1.5 miles)

This trail is part of the Rockport State Recreation Area, located near Presque Isle, Michigan. The route is a loop trail and is 1.5 miles. It is a beautiful and pleasant walk with amazing views of Lake Huron. Some of the many things that can be enjoyed while visiting this trail are hiking, walking, bird watching, and wildlife. The different seasons enhance the views of the beautiful wildflowers. Best traveled in June through October. Be prepared for mosquitos, bringing some form of insect repellent and proper clothing are suggested. There is a vault toilet at the trailhead.

Norway Ridge Trail (Easy, 7 miles, Elevation gain 131 ft)

This trail is located in Alpena, Michigan and is part of the Thunder Bay River State Forest. The route type is a loop and is 7 miles. Some of the many things that can be enjoyed while visiting this trail are hiking, mountain biking, bird watching, wildflowers and wildlife. The trail is especially beautiful during the fall season with the amazing colors. Be prepared for mosquitos, bringing some form of insect repellent and proper clothing are suggested.

Algonquin and Chippewa Loop (Easy, 6.6 miles, Elevation gain 52 ft)

This trail is near Black River, Michigan and is part of Negwegon State Park. The route type is a loop and is 6.6 miles. It goes through wooded areas with a variety of tree types and along the rocky shores of Lake

Huron. Some of the many things that can be enjoyed while visiting this trail are hiking, running, camping, and wildlife. The different seasons enhance the views of the beautiful wildflowers and forest. Be prepared for mosquitos, bringing some form of insect repellent and proper clothing are suggested. Pets are allowed on a leash. It is important to verify online and check if your pet will be able to handle the distance and terrain that will be encountered. Michigan Recreation Passport is required for vehicle entry. Vault toilets are available in the parking area.

Green Point Dunes Nature Preserve Trail (Moderate, 1.7 miles, Elevation gain 390 ft)

This trail is located near Frankfort, Michigan. The route type is a loop and is 1.7 miles. The trail goes through the woods and meadows. Depending on when you visit, there are wild flowers to enjoy and various birds to see. There is an awesome view of Lake Michigan and the beach. Some of the many things that can be enjoyed while visiting this trail are hiking, bird watching, wildlife, cross-country skiing and snowshoeing. The ideal times to visit are May through October. Pets are allowed on a leash.

Overlook Trail (Easy, 1 mile, Elevation gain 78 ft)

This trail is located near Arcadia, Michigan and is part of the Arcadia Dunes: C.S. Mott Nature Preserve. The route is an out and back type and is just 1 mile. There is an amazing view of Lake Michigan that you will be able to enjoy while on this trail. The different seasons enhance the beautiful views of Lake Michigan and the forest.

Pete's Woods Trail (Easy, 1.5 miles, Elevation gain 160 ft)

This trail is located near Arcadia, Michigan in Arcadia Dunes: C.S. Mott Nature Preserve and is a loop route that is 1.5 miles. It goes along a forested ridge and is hilly. A beautiful quiet walk with various bird sightings to enjoy. If you have the opportunity to visit this trail in May, there should be plenty of beautiful Spring wildflowers, including Trillium. Some of the many things that can be enjoyed while visiting this trail are hiking, walking, bird watching and wildlife.

AuSable River Trail (Easy, 3.2 miles, Elevation gain 88 ft)

This trail is in Hartwick Pines State Park near Grayling, Michigan. The route type is a loop and is 3.2 miles. Some of the many things that can be enjoyed while visiting this trail are hiking, running, wildflowers, and wildlife. Pets are allowed on a leash. Michigan Recreation Passport is required for vehicle entry.

Old Growth Forest Trail (Easy, 1.4 miles, Elevation gain 72 ft)

This paved trail is in Hartwick Pines State Park near Grayling, Michigan. The route type is a loop and is 1.4 miles. Some of the many things that can be enjoyed while visiting this trail are walking, bird watching, wildflowers, and wildlife. Pets are allowed on a leash. Michigan Recreation Passport is required for vehicle entry.

Manistee River Trail via Red Bridge to Seaton Creek Campground (Moderate, 10.3 miles, Elevation gain 849 ft)

This trail is in the Manistee National Forest, near Harrietta, Michigan. The route type is point to point along the Manistee River. It is possible to camp along the way and make the trip back to your starting point, or have a car at the end location. This is a beautiful trail and will be enhanced during the fall season with all the wonderful colors. Some of the many things that can be enjoyed while visiting this trail are hiking, fishing, backpacking, camping, wildflowers, and wildlife. Pets are allowed on a leash.

Southern Lower Peninsula Trails

Bald Mountain North Unit Trails- White and Orange Trail Double Loop (Moderate, 5.2 miles, Elevation gain 321 ft)

This trail is in Bald Mountain State Recreation Area, near Rochester, Michigan. The route type is a loop and is 5.2 miles. Depending on the time of year there may be some muddy areas on the trail. Some of the many things that can be enjoyed while visiting this trail are hiking, running, mountain biking, and cross-country skiing. The different seasons enhance the views of the lake, river, and forest. Be prepared for mosquitos, woods and water are a combination that mosquitos may be an issue. Bringing some form of insect repellent is suggested. Pets are allowed on a leash. Michigan Recreation Passport is required for vehicle entry.

Holly State Recreation Area Wilderness Trail (Moderate, 5.7 miles, Elevation gain 416 ft)

This trail is in the Holly Recreation Area, near Holly Michigan. The route type is a loop and is 5.7 miles. The different seasons can enhance the beautiful views of the lakes and woods. Some of the many things that can be enjoyed while visiting this trail are hiking, running, mountain biking, wildlife, wildflowers and forest. Be prepared for mosquitos, woods and water are a combination that mosquitos may be an issue. Bringing some form of insect repellent is suggested. Pets are allowed on a leash. Michigan Recreation Passport is required for vehicle entry.

Homestead Trail (Moderate, 2.1 miles, Elevation gain 164 ft)

This trail is located in P.J. Hoffmaster State Park near Muskegon, Michigan. The route type is a loop and is 2.1 miles. A portion of the trail is a beach walk on the beautiful Lake Michigan shoreline. Some of the many things that can be enjoyed while visiting this trail are hiking, running, bird watching and wildlife. At the time of putting this guide together, parts of the trail are temporarily closed. This may cause you to backtrack a little. It is still a beautiful hike with views of the sand dunes and Lake Michigan. Contacting the park before your trip will be helpful to choose the direction to go on the trail. Michigan Recreation Passport is required for vehicle entry. Restrooms are available in the day-use area on Lake Michigan.

Maybury Hiking Trail Loop (Easy, 3.1 miles, Elevation gain 127 ft)

This trail is in Maybury State Park, near Northville, Michigan. The route type is a loop and is 3.1 miles. Some of the many things that can be enjoyed while visiting this trail are hiking, running, wildlife, wildflowers and forest. Pets are allowed on a leash. Michigan Recreation Passport is required for vehicle entry.

Potawatomi Trail - Half Loop (Moderate, 13.7 miles, Elevation gain 971 ft)

This trail is part of the Pinckney Recreation Area, near Dexter, Michigan. The route is a loop type and is 13.7 miles. This is a popular trail for bikers as well. Be sure to hike the trail counterclockwise, the mountain bikers are directed to go clockwise. Some of the many things that can be enjoyed while visiting this trail are hiking, walking, mountain biking, and bird watching. The different seasons enhance the beautiful views of the lake, river and forest. Be prepared for mosquitos, bringing some form of insect repellent and proper clothing are suggested. Pets are allowed on a leash. It is important to verify online and check if your pet will be able to handle the distance and terrain that will be encountered. Restrooms are available at the trailhead near Silver Lake. Michigan Recreation Passport is required for vehicle entry.

Seven Lakes Loop (Moderate, 4.1 miles, Elevation gain 177 ft)

This trail is located in Seven Lakes State Park, near Holly Michigan. The route type is a loop and is 4.1 miles. Beautiful trail of the lakes that is enhanced with the fall colors. Depending on the season and weather, it can be a bit muddy. Some of the many things that can be enjoyed while visiting this trail are hiking, running, mountain biking, fishing, camping, bird watching and wildlife. Be prepared for mosquitos, bringing some form of insect repellent and proper clothing are suggested. Pets are allowed on a leash. Michigan Recreation Passport is required for vehicle entry.

Woldumar Nature Center Loop (Moderate, 3.1 miles, Elevation gain 91 ft)

This trail is near Dimondale, Michigan. The route type is a loop and is 3.1 miles. There is a small donation entrance fee per person, currently only $2. The trail maps are available at the Visitor center. This is a beautiful trail with a variety of wild flowers, wetlands and trees. Be prepared for mosquitos, woods and water are a combination that mosquitos may be an issue. Bringing some form of insect repellent is suggested. Pets are allowed on a leash. Some of the many things that can be enjoyed while visiting this trail are bird watching, hiking and running. The Woldumar Nature Center is open year-round.

Eastern Upper Peninsula Trails

Upper and Lower Tahquamenon Falls (Moderate, 10.2 miles, Elevation gain 636 ft)

This trail is located near Paradise, Michigan. The route type is out and back and is 10.2 miles. The Tahquamenon Falls are a beautiful site to see. Whatever season you visit this trail, you will have an amazing variety of colors to enjoy. If this trail is too long, there are shorter trails to see these beautiful Falls individually. Some of the many things that can be enjoyed while visiting this trail are hiking, fishing, wildlife and wildflowers. April through October are the best times to go on this trail. Be prepared for mosquitos, woods and water are a combination that mosquitos may be an issue. Bringing some form of insect repellent is suggested. Pets are allowed on a leash. It is important to verify online and check if your pet will be able to handle the distance and terrain that will be encountered. Restrooms are available near the Upper and Lower Falls. Michigan Recreation Passport is required for vehicle entry.

Tahquamenon Falls Upper Falls Loop (Easy, 1.5 miles, Elevation gain 183 ft)

This trail is located near Paradise, Michigan. The route type is a loop and is 1.5-mile. This trail is mostly paved with some stairs along the way. The Tahquamenon Falls are a beautiful site to see. Whatever season you visit this trail, you will have an amazing variety of colors to enjoy. Some of the many things that can be enjoyed while visiting this trail are hiking, bird watching, wildlife and wildflowers. April through October are the best times to go on this trail. Be prepared for mosquitos, woods and water are a combination that mosquitos may be an issue. Bringing some form of insect repellent is suggested. Pets are allowed on a leash. Restrooms are available near the Falls. Michigan Recreation Passport is required for vehicle entry.

Tahquamenon Falls Upper Falls Nature Trail (Easy, 1 mile, Elevation gain 59 ft)

This trail is located near Newberry, Michigan. The route type is out and back and is 1 mile. This trail is paved and leads to an observation deck. The Upper Tahquamenon Falls can be viewed through the trees. This trail avoids stairs for those that want to enjoy the beautiful view and are unable to traverse stairs. Whichever season you visit this trail, you will have an amazing variety of colors to experience. Some of the many things that can be enjoyed while visiting this trail are hiking and bird watching. April through October are the best times to go on this trail. Be prepared for mosquitos, woods and water are a combination that mosquitos may be an issue. Bringing some form of insect repellent is suggested. Pets are allowed on a leash. Restrooms are available near the Falls. Michigan Recreation Passport is required for vehicle entry.

Lower Tahquamenon Falls (Moderate, 3.2 miles, Elevation gain 200 ft)

This trail is located near Paradise, Michigan. The route type is a loop and is 3.2-mile. It is a dirt and gravel trail with some areas of wooden boardwalks. This trail is open year round. The Lower Tahquamenon Falls are beautiful, especially in the autumn months. Whatever season you visit this trail, you will have an amazing variety of colors to enjoy. Some of the many things that can be enjoyed while visiting the trail are hiking, bird watching, camping and wildlife. Be prepared for mosquitos, woods and water are a combination that mosquitos may be an issue. Bringing some form of insect repellent is suggested. Pets are allowed on a leash. It is important to verify online and check if your pet will be able to handle the distance and terrain that will be encountered. Restrooms are available near the Falls. Michigan Recreation Passport is required for vehicle entry.

Clark Lake Loop Trail (Moderate, 5.2 miles, Elevation gain 134 ft)

This trail is part of Tahquamenon Falls State Park near Paradise, Michigan. The route is a loop type and is 5.2 miles and begins at the parking lot on Clark Lake Road. It is a beautiful wooded trail that takes you near Clark Lake. Best traveled in June through October. Michigan Recreation Passport is required for vehicle entry.

Sable Falls Trail (Easy, 0.6 miles, Elevation gain 101 ft)

This trail is part of the Pictured Rocks National Lakeshore. This route type is an out and back and is 0.6 miles round trip from the parking lot to the shore. The best view of Sable Falls is at the bottom of 168 steps. This route is short and has beautiful views including a sandy and rocky beach on Lake Superior. The trail is open year-round. Pets are allowed on a leash.

Western Upper Peninsula Trails

Hogback Mountain Trail (Moderate, 3.1 miles, Elevation gain 564 ft)

This trail is located near Marquette, Michigan. The route type is out and back and is 3.1-mile. Be prepared for a steep incline towards the top, using caution with your footing. There is an incredible view at the top. April through October are the best months to take this trail. Some of the many things that can be enjoyed while visiting this trail are hiking, wildflowers and wildlife. Pets are allowed on a leash. It is important to verify online and check if your pet will be able to handle the distance and terrain that will be encountered.

Presque Isle Park Loop (Easy, 2.3 miles, Elevation gain 127 ft)

This trail is near Marquette, Michigan. The route type is a loop and is 2.3 miles. The views of the cliffs and Lake Superior are beautiful. The fall colors enhance the beauty of this trail. Some of the many things that can be enjoyed while visiting this trail are hiking, walking, bird watching, fishing, running, wildlife, forest, beach, and wildflowers. This trail is best traveled March through November. Please use caution in the colder months, it may be icy. No pets are allowed. Restrooms are available near the parking area.

Wagner Falls Lookout (Easy, .25 mile)

This is a short walk if you are in the area and have time to take in the beautiful view of Wagner Falls. It is located near Munising, Michigan. Some of the many things that can be enjoyed while visiting this trail are hiking, bird watching, forest and wildlife. The parking lot is small. Please use caution when entering and exiting the parking lot, M94 curves in this area. Pets are allowed on a leash.

Chapel Loop- Mosquito Falls and Chapel Falls (Moderate, 10.2 miles, Elevation gain 754 ft)

This trail is part of the Pictured Rocks National Lakeshore, near Munising, Michigan. The route type is a loop and is 10.2 miles. This is a popular route for hiking and camping. There are seasonal road closures, it is best to check online while planning the trip. Be prepared for mosquitos, woods and water are a combination that mosquitos may be an issue. Bringing some form of insect repellent is suggested. The prime months to plan this trip are April through November. If Chapel loop is too long, there are shorter trails listed in this book to visit these falls. Pets are not allowed.

Chapel Falls and Chapel Beach (Moderate, 6.8 miles, Elevation gain 410 ft)

This trail is located near Shingleton, Michigan. This route type is out and back and is 6.8 miles and considered moderate. The views are beautiful, especially Chapel Rock and Lake Superior. Some of the many things that can be enjoyed while visiting this trail are hiking, wildflowers, forest and wildlife. April through October are the best months to visit this trail. To access this trail Chapel Road may require a vehicle with high clearance due to possible wet conditions. Be prepared for mosquitos, woods and water are a combination that mosquitos may be an issue. Bringing some form of insect repellent is suggested. Pets are not allowed. A seasonal vault toilet is available at the trailhead.

Mosquito Falls and Mosquito Beach Loop *(Moderate, 4.6 miles, Elevation gain 403 ft)*

This trail is located near Shingleton, Michigan. This route is a loop and is considered to be moderately challenging. The distance is 4.6 miles. The Falls are one of the smaller ones in Pictured Rocks National Lakeshore. The Beach is on the shoreline of Lake Superior. Some of the many things that can be enjoyed while visiting this trail are hiking, camping, forest and wildlife. The prime months to visit are May through October. Be prepared for mosquitos, woods and water are a combination that mosquitos may be an issue. Bringing some form of insect repellent is suggested. Pets are not allowed.

Miners Castle and Miners Beach *(Moderate, 2.8 miles, Elevation gain 252 ft)*

This trail is part of Pictured Rocks National Lakeshore and is located near Munising, Michigan. The route is out and back and is 2.8 miles. The beach is on the shoreline of beautiful Lake Superior. The trail may be muddy in the Spring, due to melting snow. Some of the many things that can be enjoyed while visiting this trail are hiking, running, river and forest. Prime months to visit are June through September. Be prepared for black flies, hikers have reported this may be an issue. Bringing some form of insect repellent is suggested. Pets are not allowed.

Beaver Lake and Little Beaver Lake *(Moderate, 5.7 miles, Elevation*

gain 301 ft)

This trail is part of Pictured Rocks National Lakeshore and is located near Shingleton, Michigan. The route is a loop trail and is 5.7 miles. Parts of the trail have views of two inland lakes, Beaver Lake and Little Beaver Lake and also Lake Superior. Some of the many things that can be enjoyed while visiting this trail are hiking, running, camping, wildflowers, wildlife, forest and Beaver Creek. Be prepared for black flies, hikers have reported this may be an issue. Bringing some form of insect repellent and proper clothing is suggested. Pets are not allowed.

Sugarloaf Mountain Trail (Moderate, 1.4 miles, Elevation gain 295 ft)

This trail is located near Marquette, Michigan. The route is a loop trail and is 1.4 miles. Please use caution with your footing, hikers have reported that there are loose rocks and roots sticking out along the trail. There is a stairway leading to a viewing platform giving a picturesque view. Some of the many things that can be enjoyed while visiting this trail are hiking, snowshoeing, wildflowers, wildlife and forest. This trail is best traveled April through October. Be prepared for mosquitos, woods and water are a combination that mosquitos may be an issue. Bringing some form of insect repellent is suggested. Pets are allowed on a leash.

Bear Lake Trail (Easy, 2.6 miles, Elevation gain 45 ft)

This trail is in McLain State Park, near Calumet, Michigan. The route type is out and back and is 2.6 miles. There are beautiful views of both Lake Superior and Bear Lake. Some of the many things that can be enjoyed while visiting this trail are hiking, running, wildflowers, fishing, bird watching, wildlife and forest. Be prepared for mosquitos, woods and water are a combination that mosquitos may be an issue. Bringing some form of insect repellent is suggested. Michigan Recreation Passport is required for vehicle entry.

McLain State Park West Loop *(Easy, 2 miles, Elevation gain 55 ft)*

This trail is located near Hancock, Michigan. The route type is a loop and is 2 miles. There are some beautiful views of Lake Superior from the rocky beach. Some of the many things that can be enjoyed while visiting this trail are hiking, cross-country skiing, snowshoeing, wildflowers, bird watching, wildlife and forest. This trail is best traveled July through August. Be prepared for mosquitos, woods and water are a combination that mosquitos may be an issue. Bringing some form of insect repellent is suggested. Michigan Recreation Passport is required for vehicle entry.

Conclusion

I hope that you will enjoy some of these trails that are in this book. There are so many more beautiful trails in Michigan that are not listed in this guide. The outdoors in Michigan have so much to offer!

If you have found this book helpful, I'd be very appreciative if you left a favorable review for the book on Amazon! Thank you!

Resources

National Park Service. (2022, December 16). *Sable Falls (U.S. National Park Service)*.
   Retrieved March 31, 2024, from https://www.nps.gov/places/sable-falls.htm

National Park Service. (2022, December 6). *Wagner Falls (U.S. National Park Service)*.
   Retrieved March 31, 2024, from https://www.nps.gov/places/wagner-falls.htm

Michigan Digital. (2024). *Michigan Trail Maps Michigan Hiking Biking and Birding Maps -*
   Michigan Trail Maps. Michigan Trail Maps. Retrieved March 31, 2024,
   from https://www.michigantrailmaps.com/

AllTrails. (2024). *Best Trails in Michigan*. AllTrails.com. Retrieved March 31, 2024,
   from https://www.alltrails.com/us/michigan

Michigan Department of Natural Resources. (2024). *Michigan Recreation Search*. Retrieved
   March 31, 2024, from https://www.michigandnr.com/parksandtrails/Default.aspx

Made in United States
North Haven, CT
23 May 2024

52831731R00020